THE PRESBYTERIAN RULING ELDER

Other titles of interest

The Presbyterian Deacon:
An Essential Guide
Revised edition
Earl S. Johnson, Jr.
978-0-664-50325-3

Presbyterian Polity for Church Leaders
Fourth edition
Joan S. Gray and Joyce C. Tucker
978-0-664-50315-4

Sailboat Church:
Helping Your Church Rethink Its Mission and Practice
Joan S. Gray
978-0-664-25958-7

Selected to Serve:
A Guide for Church Leaders
Second edition
Earl S. Johnson, Jr.
978-0-664-50317-8

Spiritual Leadership for Church Officers:
A Handbook
Joan S. Gray
978-0-664-50305-5

To order these books,
visit our Web site at www.ThePresbyterianLeader.com
or call 1–800–533–4371.

THE PRESBYTERIAN RULING ELDER

AN ESSENTIAL GUIDE

Paul S. Wright

REVISED BY
Stephens G. Lytch

Geneva Press
Louisville, Kentucky

© 2014 Geneva Press

First published as *The Duties of the Ruling Elder*, copyright 1957 by W. L. Jenkins; copyright © 1972 The Westminster Press. Revised edition published as *The Presbyterian Elder*, copyright © 1992 Geneva Press.

Revised Edition
Published by Geneva Press
Louisville, Kentucky

14 15 16 17 18 19 20 21 22 23 — 10 9 8 7 6 5 4 3 2 1

Book design by Sharon Adams
Cover design by Dilu Nicholas

Library of Congress Cataloging-in-Publication Data
Wright, Paul S.
 [Presbyterian elder]
 The Presbyterian ruling elder : an essential guide / Paul S. Wright ; revised by Stephens G. Lytch. -- Revised Edition.
     pages cm
 Rev. ed. of: The Presbyterian elder. c1992.
 ISBN 978-0-664-50330-7 (alk. paper)
1. Presbyterian Church--Government. 2. Elders (Church officers)--Presbyterian Church. I. Title.
 BX9195.W7 2014
 262'.155137--dc23

2013040871

Most Geneva Press books are available at special quantity discounts when purchased in bulk by corporations, organizations, and special-interest groups. For more information, please e-mail SpecialSales@GenevaPress.com.

Contents

Introduction

*I*f you are reading this book, you have probably been elected a ruling elder by your congregation. It may have been given to you as part of a program of training and development in which you will be involved before you are ordained by the session and installed as an active member of that session. When you were asked if your name might be placed in nomination for the office of ruling elder, you doubtless had some concerns and questions: Am I the right person? What is a ruling elder and what does he or she do? How much time will it take to serve on the session? Some of these questions may have been answered by the nominating committee; others will be answered during the time of preparation. But you consented to serve if elected because you love your church and wish to do your part in serving it.

This book is intended to provide some answers to your questions about being a ruling elder in the Presbyterian Church: what are the duties of ruling elders and how can you perform them more effectively. With the other materials you will be examining, it will help you to find satisfaction in your service to the church. You will not find all you may wish to know in these pages. There is much more to learn, and there is a wealth of resources to help you.

Since its beginnings, the Presbyterian Church has placed great emphasis on the leadership of laypersons, both as reflecting the will of God for the church and as essential for the vitality of the church. Consequently, your training, at this period and throughout your service as a ruling elder, is of prime importance. Among the most interesting aspects of the work to which you may look forward is the opportunity for self-improvement and growth as you work with your pastor and fellow leaders. Yours is an essential and important task. The Presbyterian Church holds it in honor. May you find increasing joy in the performance of your duties as a faithful servant of Jesus Christ.

Quotations from the *Book of Order* (e.g., G-2.0102) are from *The Constitution of the Presbyterian Church (U.S.A.), Part II: Book of Order* (Louisville, KY: Office of the General Assembly, Presbyterian Church (U.S.A.), 2011–2013).

Chapter 1

God Calls Persons to Serve

You are a Protestant and you belong to a particular branch of Protestantism called "Reformed." Even more particularly, you are a member of the Presbyterian Church in that family of Reformed churches. This particularity makes a big difference when you, as a layperson, seek to define your relationship to the church. You may have taken it quite for granted that as a church member you are called on to teach in the education program, to serve on committees that determine the programs of your church, to assist the pastor in parish visitation, or to perform the many other tasks necessary to the ministry and mission of your congregation. You may have participated in worship as a liturgist, preacher, or member of the choir. Whatever part you may have taken in the life of your church, you have correctly assumed, because you are a Christian and a church member, that you have the right and duty to be more than a spectator or a passive recipient of work done by "professionals." In a very real sense, laypersons are the church.

Let us take this thought a little further. Is the distinction we commonly make between laypersons and clergy a valid one? Certainly in such fields of human endeavor as medicine or law it is valid to differentiate between laypersons and professionals. Doctors and lawyers have specialized knowledge and skills that the rest of us do not possess, and we would be foolish not to recognize and avail ourselves of their competencies. But is this true also in matters of religion?

There are hierarchical churches that teach that this distinction must be recognized within church order. They hold that two orders of believers were created by Christ: a clerical order, with a unique status in relation to God, and a lay order, which stands in an inferior and different position ecclesiastically and functionally in the church. According to this concept there are gradations of spiritual authority, conferred by the rite of ordination into the succession of the apostles, in order that the church might be infallibly guided in all that pertains to right doctrine and moral living. All this is seen as a divine provision for the proper government of the church and for the nurture of the flock of God.

It is obvious that this is not the concept or practice of the Protestant church, and in particular it is not the way of the Presbyterian Church. The Form of Government of the Presbyterian Church (U.S.A.) states that "the Church's ordered ministries described in the New Testament and maintained by this church are deacons and presbyters (teaching elders and ruling elders)" (G-2.0102). It may sometimes appear that there are two classes of people in the church—ministers and laypersons—but our constitution makes it clear that ministry, the work of the church, is one ministry. The difference between "lay" and "clergy" lies in particular functions performed by those who are ordained. "The existence of these ordered ministries [ruling elders, teaching elders, and deacons] in no way diminishes the importance of the commitment of all members to the total ministry of the Church" (G-2.0102).

Teaching elders must fulfill certain academic and other requirements (see G-2.06), including four years of college and three years of theological study while in covenant relationship with session and presbytery as inquirers and candidates. They are then ordained to a call by presbytery and perform certain functions that other persons do not, in particular the administration of the sacraments and moderating the session. If there is a valid distinction between "lay" and "clergy," it is at this point.

For Presbyterian Protestants, the following two things are clear regarding the relationship of clergy and laypersons.

1. Priesthood is a vocation of every member of the church. Each believer is a priest. "Members and those in ordered ministries serve together under the mandate of Christ" (G-2.0101). We may all come to God without benefit of an intermediary because Christ is our Mediator. We may make our confessions and receive forgiveness by that right, which our Lord has bestowed on us. At the same time, all believers are to serve a priestly function to each other. In his pastoral letter, James exhorts believers to "confess your sins to one another, and pray for one another, so that you may be healed" (Jas. 5:16). Each person who is a forgiven sinner may be the channel of God's grace to another sinner who is seeking God's forgiveness and peace. Indeed, this loving service may be more effectively performed by a spiritually experienced Christian who is a friend than by a pastor. A part of our calling to be Christian bestows this privilege on us.

The priesthood of all believers underlies the worship of a Protestant church. Worship is a corporate act in which all participate and in which each participant helps the other. This is particularly evident at the Lord's Table, where the one presiding points to Jesus Christ as the host. With the people, the one presiding gives thanks for the gifts of bread and wine and sets them apart for their sacred use. The elements are passed from person to person as dramatic evidence of the truth that we have one Redeemer and that we are all brothers and sisters. As persons partake of the bread and wine, they are led by the Holy Spirit to discern the *real* within the symbol, to offer their own and others' needs to God, and to receive enabling grace. The emphasis is on the conversation between each soul and Christ, who is really present by faith. Thus each acts as his or her own priest, in partaking, and as priest to others, in passing the elements and in praying for others.

The priesthood of all believers is most obvious in worship in the sacrament of the Lord's Supper, but it exists in other parts of worship as well. Martin Luther observed that congregational singing is a priestly service in which each worshiper helps others to praise God. Greeting each other with an offering of God's peace and sharing mutual concerns and joys in prayer are means of grace within common worship. Leading our families in worship in the home and interceding with love for friends, neighbors, and those in need of God's grace are special ways in which every believer acts as priest. When we are what we ought to be, every believer in Christ is one through whom others may come to God and God's grace may be poured out on them.

2. This relationship between persons in the Presbyterian Church is also seen in our concept of ordination. By ordination we refer to a religious rite practiced certainly from very early times in the Christian church (Acts 6:6; 13:3; 1 Tim. 4:14; 5:22). It is based on the conviction that the Holy Spirit bestows gifts on believers for the common good (1 Cor. 12:4–11). We acknowledge these gifts of special tasks and skills by ordaining, or "setting apart" through the laying on of hands, certain persons to orders in the church. Thus distinctions that may be made in the Presbyterian system are based on functions and on the recognition of those special gifts bestowed by the Holy Spirit that are to be used for the good of all.

Teaching elders are "responsible for a quality of life and relationships that commends the gospel to all persons and that communicates its joy and justice. They are responsible for studying, teaching, and preaching the Word, for celebrating Baptism and the Lord's Supper, and for praying with and for the congregation" (G-2.0504). Most of these duties are to be shared with others, specifically with ruling elders and deacons, and this section of the *Book of Order,* G-2.0504, goes on to indicate how this is to be done.

> Ruling elders are so named not because they "lord it over" the congregation (Matt. 20:25), but because they are chosen by the congregation to discern and measure its fidelity to the Word of God and to strengthen and nurture its faith and life. Ruling elders, together with teaching elders, exercise leadership, government, spiritual discernment, and discipline and have responsibilities for the life of a congregation as well as the whole church, including ecumenical relationships. (G-2.0301)
>
> The ministry of deacon as set forth in Scripture is one of compassion, witness, and service, sharing the redeeming love of Jesus Christ for the poor, the hungry, the sick, the lost, the friendless, the oppressed, those burdened by unjust policies or structures, or anyone in distress. (G-2.0201)

Since we are concerned in this book with the work of the ruling elder, let us look for a moment at some points of similarity and difference between the orders of ruling elder and teaching elder. As presbyters (those having governance and serving as members of councils in the church), ruling elders and teaching elders have equal standing. The vote of ruling elders in sessions, presbyteries, synods, and General Assemblies counts just as much as does that of teaching elders. General Assembly is made up of equal numbers of ruling elders and teaching elders, and in presbyteries and synods the numbers are approximately equal. Obviously, there is little if any distinction made between the two orders in the governance of the church. On the contrary, there is significant parity between them. This is important in the life of the Presbyterian Church.

But there are differences. Ruling elders do not labor in "Word and doctrine." This is required of teaching elders, who are also called ministers of the Word and Sacrament, and if it is to be done in a fitting and profitable manner, requires special training and faithful preparation (2 Tim. 2:15). Teaching elders will, therefore, ordinarily be more skilled in preaching and teaching the Word. Indeed, such persons may be said to have been called by the Holy Spirit to this vocation, for which academic discipline is intended to make them worthy workers. So by divine call and by training, the teaching elder occupies a position of unique value and responsibility in relation to the flock of Christ. Teaching elders are honored and respected not because of any attributes or powers within themselves, but because of the calling of God and the training they have received for their work.

Our Reformed heritage causes us to take a dim view of "professionalism" and "specialists" in matters of faith. Faith is an encounter with God. The truth of the Christian faith is not some secret learning to which only certain initiates have access; neither is it a spiritual power that only some possess and can transmit. The heart of our faith is that Christ comes to persons whom the Spirit has awakened to faith. It is a perversion to think of our faith in terms of "professionalism." We would not tolerate professionals responsible for praying for us any more than we would tolerate professionals responsible for showing Christian love. The church is true to itself and its Lord when there are *not* two classes of people—one with a unique status in relation to the things of God and another standing in an inferior position.

Now let us look briefly at the history of the Christian church so that we may be reminded how, from its beginning, laypersons have been inherently a part of its order and life.

The New Testament provides ample evidence that God calls laypersons to labor in and through the church. Immediately we think of those whom Jesus chose to be with him, none of them members of the religious establishment. Peter was a fisherman, Matthew a tax gatherer. Except for Nicodemus, no rulers of the synagogue or of the temple hierarchy are mentioned among those close to Jesus. It is significant that he chose lay women and men who had a capacity for growth and loyalty and who were willing to give themselves courageously to a spiritual mission. This is another example of how God bypasses the establishment in order to get on with God's purpose in the world.

The same evidence is found in the Old Testament. With few exceptions, the prophets and other leaders were laypersons, chosen by God for the often difficult and dangerous task of calling the people back to the path God had chosen for them. There is an openness of heart to the Spirit of the living God that is characteristic of those whom God chooses for places of leadership and responsibility.

After the death and resurrection of Christ, there was little sign of formal organization among his followers. Peter seems to have been their accepted spokesperson, but as he began his missionary journeys it was James, Jesus' brother, who assumed leadership in the Christian community in Jerusalem. In the beginning, the company of believers continued to live and worship very much as they had before Jesus came. They worshiped in the Temple and doubtless attended the synagogues. But as their numbers grew and they were scattered throughout Palestine and abroad, they were more and more excluded from the synagogue fellowship. As the Christians grew more conscious of their new identity in Christ, they found themselves becoming separate from Judaism. The strong leadership of Paul and the rapid spread of Christianity among the Gentiles hastened this process. Consequently, the small communities of Christians throughout the cities and towns of the Roman Empire began to organize themselves, usually around the pattern of the synagogue with which they were familiar.

The synagogue was a democratic institution that had come into being at the time of the destruction of the Temple and the captivity of Israel in Babylon. It came to have such importance to the Jews scattered in communities around the Roman Empire that, even after the restoration of

Temple worship in Jerusalem, these synagogues continued to have a major role in fostering religious life. Mention is frequently made in the New Testament of the "elders of the synagogue." These were probably older men whose prestige among the people elevated them to positions of oversight and trust. Leadership was often a function of age and experience. Even in the Roman senate and elsewhere, the rulers of the people, judges, and magistrates, were selected from among the elderly. In time the title "elder" was applied to certain leaders regardless of the age of the person.

When, as we have said, Christians became separated from the Jewish community and began to form communities of their own, they patterned both their worship and their organization after that of the synagogue. Thus, just as there had been elders in the synagogue who were entrusted with rule and order as well as the teaching of the people, so in the early Christian communities elders were appointed by the founders of the churches or chosen by the people themselves. The responsibilities of these persons were particularly heavy because the original apostles became fewer in number with the passing of the years, and they devoted most of their time to missionary work. Those who were trained and appointed by the apostles as preachers and teachers also traveled from place to place, founding new congregations and making converts. When these persons were not present, the nurture and discipline of the congregation fell on the shoulders of the elders. Naturally they came to be persons who were highly esteemed and invaluable to the church.

The measure of respect and confidence in which they were held by the apostle Paul is evident in the touching story in Acts 20:17–38, where he summons the elders of the church in Ephesus to Miletus for a conference and a parting word of encouragement and farewell. It is impossible to measure how much of the spread and the continuing strength of the early church was due to the efforts of these early elders. It was they who preserved, in large part, the integrity of the faith and who, in times of persecution, rallied the flock to stand firm.

In the centuries that followed, this democratic, lay-administered organization of the church gradually weakened. As the church grew in numbers and importance, there developed a hierarchical structure in which the administration of the church and its work of preaching, teaching, and worship were placed more and more in the hands of the clergy. The consequence was that laity were excluded from all responsible participation in and direction of religious activities. The lay movement did not die out, however. Certain lay orders arose within the church and fostered a life of piety and good deeds. These communities of humble faith and service kept alive a genuine spiritual glow during centuries we sometimes call the Dark Ages. To them also we owe the preservation of the Scriptures and much of the art, music, liturgy, and sense of mission and ministry that belong to Christ's church.

At the beginning of the sixteenth century, the time was ripe for change and renewal. With reforms in politics, economics, and learning came a corresponding religious movement known as the Reformation. The purpose of its leaders was not to start a new church but to cleanse the existing institution of abuses and impurities. It was sparked by a rediscovery of the faith of the early Christians to which the New Testament bore witness. For our purposes we shall confine our story to the Reformation in Geneva, Switzerland, of which John Calvin was the leader. The beginnings of the Presbyterian system of doctrine and church government lie there.

For his organizational model, Calvin used the church of the second century. We have mentioned that there is little in the New Testament or in other historical material about the organization of the very early church. Indeed, there seems to have been little in the way of formal organization among the early companies of Christians. They held that the Holy Spirit distributed gifts among the faithful to be used to benefit the whole group (1 Cor. 12:4–11), and the whole congregation assumed responsibility for its own order and discipline as its circumstances and location demanded. A better-articulated system developed during the second century. Calvin held that Christ had instituted in the church the four offices of pastor, teacher, ruling elder, and deacon. Pastors were to preach the Word of God, teachers were to establish schools for the education of the young and the instruction of adults (the beginning of the public school system and the Presbyterian emphasis on Christian education), ruling elders were to maintain order and discipline, and deacons were to administer charities for the relief of the poor and destitute.

In Calvin's Geneva, the ruling elders were laymen, twelve in number, who represented the various parishes in the city and related both to the church and to the civil government. They took an oath similar to that prescribed for ministers. They met once each week with the pastors in a body known as the consistory to hear complaints against immoralities, indecent language, doctrinal error, or other matters that might corrupt the purity of the church and bring reproach on its good name. At the end of the year the elders presented themselves to the magistrates, who decided whether they had faithfully performed their duties and should be kept in office.

Here we have the elements characteristic of Presbyterian ecclesiastical life and discipline. Here were ministers and laity with equal authority but who, with a division of responsibility and labor, served the church for its edification and order. The system was somewhat modified when this family of the Reformation spread beyond Geneva. Civil authority became much less closely tied to the church, and ruling elders came to be elected by members of the congregation and not appointed by the councils of municipal government. Yet they continued to be entrusted with the "peace, unity, and purity" of the church, and so, to distinguish their office from that of pastors, they were called "ruling elders."

From Geneva, Calvin's Reformation spread to Scotland, to northern Ireland, to Holland, and from the Old World to the New. During this migration it never lost the essentials of its ecclesiastical structure. In any Presbyterian church, regardless of size or location, the session is the superior authority charged with responsibility for the whole life of the congregation. Teaching elders and ruling elders—both ordained—work together under the guidance of the Holy Spirit to present every person "mature in Christ" (Col. 1:28).

Chapter 2

Who Qualifies to Be a Ruling Elder?

Sue was proud and happy that her church had just elected her as a ruling elder. It was gratifying that this confidence had been placed in her. She had grown up in the church, taught in the church school, and served on the youth council of the presbytery. She had expressed some doubts when the nominating committee visited with an invitation to allow her name to be placed on the ballot. After the committee members left, she had called her father, who was also a ruling elder. He was delighted at her news. "Your question is the same as mine when I was first asked," he told her. "Am I good enough to be an elder?"

At the time Sue was twenty-two years old. Perhaps her youth had something to do with her doubts. As we noted in the first chapter, from earliest times in every society, the old men have been asked to give counsel and leadership to the people; hence the term "elder." Sue was not sure she had had sufficient experience or the wisdom she would need to be a ruling elder and give spiritual leadership to others.

But in the matter of age, society—and the church with it—has changed considerably in its viewpoint. The performance and insights of young people who are open to the leading of the Holy Spirit and who wish to serve others are impressive and convincing. Both the constitution of the church and its practice urge that they contribute their talents through ordered ministry. Years have relatively little to do with being "good enough" to be a ruling elder. Right qualifications are not paced by the calendar. The church has found that it is greatly to its advantage to avail itself of the gifts and services of its younger members.

Additionally, the contribution of women to effective leadership in the church has been amply demonstrated as they have served as ruling elders and teaching elders. In the years since the church has permitted their ordination we have realized the truth of the apostle Paul's statement that in Christ "there is no longer male or female, for all of you are one in Christ Jesus" (Gal. 3:28).

Of more immediate pertinence, however, are two other considerations: What must a ruling elder *believe*, and what must a ruling elder *be*? In this chapter we shall consider the first.

What Must a Ruling Elder Believe?

The constitution of the church requires, at the time of ordination of elders, that nine questions be put to the candidates to which affirmative answers are required. The first three questions deal with one's personal religious faith, the last six with the duties of the elder (W-4.4003). A careful reading of the questions dealing with personal faith serves to indicate what a ruling elder must believe.

The first question is about Jesus Christ: "Do you trust in Jesus Christ your Savior, acknowledge him Lord of all and Head of the Church, and through him believe in one God, Father, Son, and Holy Spirit?" (W-4.4003a).

Central to the identity of all Christians is faith in Jesus Christ. The earliest of the creeds was probably the simple statement "Jesus is Lord." Thus those who are set apart by ordination are required to affirm their commitment to Christ. He is the one who, born in human flesh, shared our life fully. He is the one that we confess to be the true and complete revelation of God. In Christ we discover the meaning and purpose of all that God intends for human life.

Presbyterians, along with all other Christians, are monotheists and Trinitarians. By monotheists we mean that we conceive of God as one and not many. God, as Father, Son, and Holy Spirit, is not three gods, but one God. Yet Christians differ from other monotheists (Jews and Muslims) in their idea of the nature of the unity that is God. The idea that the "three are one" may sound like an impossible dilemma to some, and because it is hard and superficially illogical there have been those, like the Unitarians, who have been willing to abandon the doctrine of the Trinity. But throughout the history of the church there has been a stubborn insistence that within the unity of God there is a rich, if unfathomable, differentiation that we name "Father, Son, and Holy Spirit."

This doctrine is not the invention of theologians; indeed, it is not an invention at all. It was formulated out of the experience of those who, through the ages, were confronted by the living God. The overpowering religious experience came first, followed by the effort to define the experience in terms of doctrine. There are depths in the nature of God that finite creatures will never fully know, for God is infinite. Yet the revelation of God that we know through God's dealings with humankind is authentic and many-sided. These are the data on which our understanding of God rests. In trying to interpret them, we arrive at the doctrine of the Trinity. The clue to understanding the doctrine is the question, "How has God actually been revealed in human experience?" The Bible provides source material for an answer.

The writer of the book of Hebrews declared that "God spoke to our ancestors in many and various ways by the prophets" (Heb. 1:1). God did not speak in audible words but in mighty deeds. The revelation that God gave was not only information about God's own nature but also the way in which God's living presence was perceived in acts by those whose hearts had been opened by the Spirit of God (Eph. 1:18). To such enlightened persons the creation spoke of the "glory of God" and the firmament showed God's "handiwork" (Ps. 19:1). God's purpose was read in certain acts in history, notably in the redemption of Israel from bondage in

Egypt and the experiences incident to the settling of Canaan. We have no universally convincing explanation of why the prophets of Israel discerned in the events of their history the hand of God, but they each attributed to those events the work of the supreme Sovereign, one who was all holy, all wise, and all just. We do not know how they came to believe that the destiny of the world and of their own people in particular was to be found in God's will to rule in righteousness and mercy. What is clear from the Bible is that this idea was firmly fixed in their view of things and that it explained for them the meaning both of past events and of the future yet to be. Faith in the one true God inspired confidence in the covenant God had made with their people and the expectation that God would bless them as they sought to be a blessing to all people.

The same writer of Hebrews then goes on to say, "But in these last days [God] has spoken to us by a Son, whom [God] appointed the heir of all things, through whom [God] also created the worlds" (Heb. 1:2). The writers of the New Testament were convinced that in telling the story of Jesus they were proclaiming the greatest of the mighty events in history, in which the eternal purpose of God to visit and redeem God's people had transpired (Luke 1:68). They called their proclamation the "gospel" because it was the good news that in Jesus Christ the living God was present in their midst, bringing forgiveness of sins and salvation in new life. They did not write about Jesus as though he were another messenger who brought new tidings about God, although this is certainly a part of what he did; but they declared that, in the person, the life, the death, the resurrection, and the ascension into glory of Jesus, God had achieved salvation, bringing reconciliation and triumph over sin and death. Jesus was God's deed!

Writer after writer, preacher after preacher in the New Testament found the experience of Jesus so overwhelming that language was too poor a vehicle to express the joy and adoration awakened by it (Eph. 1:3; 1 Pet. 1:3–4; 1 John 4:9). Each reveals a spirit of joy and triumph that pervades the New Testament. But even more, each writer points to the source of that joy and confidence as the salvation event that is inseparably united with the person and work of Christ. They were so possessed by the wonder of what God had done in Christ and so engrossed in proclaiming the good news that they had no time to theologize about it; that task was left to later generations. But a new dimension within the being of God had been opened to them in the person of Jesus, and henceforth in their minds and hearts Jesus Christ and God were one within the bounds of a uniquely divine relationship.

The words in which they reported their experience and declared their faith might lead us to surmise that after his resurrection and ascension Jesus was no longer among them. They preached that he was in heaven "seated at the right hand of God" (see Mark 16:19; Heb. 1:3). Jesus was given the "name that is above every name" and was to be called

"Lord" (Phil. 2:9–11). Yet it is important to remember that even as they ascribed honor and power to him, they did not conceive of him as absent from them. On the contrary, their deepest conviction was that "I am with you always, to the end of the age" (Matt. 28:20).

The real but unseen presence of Christ among his followers was attributed by them to the sending of the Spirit. The Spirit did not take the place of Christ but enabled his followers to realize that Christ had never left them. The Lord continued to be among his disciples in the reality of his spiritual presence, through which he continued to teach them and to empower them for effective witness and right living. They believed that the Holy Spirit had been the means by which the prophets had discerned God in the events of history. The language of writers in both the New and Old Testaments leads us to assume that they did not differentiate between their experience of God realized as actively present and the influence of the Holy Spirit. Yet the Spirit is not confused with God or with Christ, from whom the Spirit is sent.

Here then is a threefold experience of the divine, which is at the same time one. We can make no sense of the doctrine of the Trinity unless we too have experienced God's reconciling the world to God in Christ and effecting reconciliation in our hearts through God's Spirit. The logic of the doctrine is in religious experience. We may try to penetrate the mystery of the "three in one," but we are better off simply to affirm that though we cannot know the depths of the being of

God, we can experience God's justice, God's salvation, and God's living presence.

The second question concerns the Scriptures: "Do you accept the Scriptures of the Old and New Testaments to be, by the Holy Spirit, the unique and authoritative witness to Jesus Christ in the Church universal, and God's Word to you?" (W-4.4003b).

What does it mean to accept the Scriptures of the Old and New Testaments as God's word to you? This involves us in the consideration of what we mean by the "word of God." Certainly we do not mean literally a written document or an audible message directly from God to a human being. When we read, "The word of the Lord came to the prophet saying . . . ," there is no description as to how the word was received. It is sometimes declared to have come through dreams or visions, which in earlier times were thought to be the media through which God communicated to humanity. Usually, however, the word of God came in connection with some important crisis in the life of the individual or the nation. As we reflect on the experiences of God's people as told in the Bible, we may infer that the "Word" was God personally present and active in a situation whose meaning was discerned by the prophet, who was also involved by the work of the Spirit. Thus God "spoke," both in the event and in the divine significance discerned by the prophet. What was "seen" or "heard" was preached as the Word of the Lord. In words, the prophets declared the Word. When these were finally written they became a part of the Bible. The ordination question refers to the Word as being the unique and authoritative witness to Jesus Christ. For all Christians, Jesus Christ is the living Word of God. In him the creative Word by which God made the universe, the eternal Reality that is the source of mind and freedom in humankind, was personally present. The Word of God is Person. All that the New Testament says about Christ, it says about the Word. Thus the question asks us to differentiate between the Word of God and words about the Word that are found in the Bible and that witness to the living Word.

A further observation must be made, however. Except for the Old Testament, we have no record of the way in which God communicated God's purposes and will for the redemption of humankind through specific acts related to the people whom God called and with whom God covenanted. Nor have we, except for the New Testament, any record of the continuation and climactic fulfillment in Jesus Christ of this same redemptive work of God. The relation between the word of God and the Scriptures is not accidental. The living Word awakened and inspired the writers of the Bible and ever since has illuminated the hearts and incited response in those who read it. We read Scripture in order to discern in its words the very word of God—God's word to us.

Truth is the supreme authority in faith and practice. We Presbyterian Protestants find that truth in the living Word to which the Scriptures testify. The living Word, who is God, known to us in Jesus Christ through the Holy Spirit, stands above every other authority. By this Word the church is judged, recognizes its need for reforming, seeks God's peace, reforms both itself and other human institutions, stands with all who are oppressed, and looks always to its Savior and Head as it seeks to embody Christ in God's world.

The third question reads: "Do you sincerely receive and adopt the essential tenets of the Reformed faith as expressed in the confessions of our church as authentic and reliable expositions of what Scripture leads us to believe and do, and will you be instructed and led by those confessions as you lead the people of God?" (W-4.4003c).

The Presbyterian Church is a confessional church. Through the years, Christians in various places and circumstances have said strongly what they believe about God, about the church, about humankind, and about the activity of God and God's people in the world that is God's. Thus our confessions are important, particularly to those of us who have been called to serve as leaders.

The Foundations of Presbyterian Polity indicates the importance of the confessions when it states, "In these statements the church declares to its members and to the world who and what it is, what it believes, and what it resolves to do. These statements identify the church as a community of people known by its convictions as well as by its actions" (F-2.01).

The Book of Confessions is a collection of statements of faith in the form of declarations, catechisms, creeds, and confessions made by the church throughout history. Each was formed in a time when the church faced a crisis and found it necessary to declare what it believed. The church reformed its life and mission as required by the will of God, revealed by the Holy Spirit through the living Word. These confessional statements unite us with those who have gone before us and whose collective experience of the living God guides our own understanding of who we are, what we believe, and what we will do in God's name. Thus the confessions are more than historical documents. "They guide the church in its study and interpretation of the Scriptures; they summarize the essence of Reformed Christian tradition; they direct the church in maintaining sound doctrines; they equip the church for its work of proclamation" (F-2.01). In receiving these confessions we admit their value and accept their guidance. In adopting them, we attempt to make them our own and form our faith and ministry from them in our own day.

It is important to note that these are referred to as "essential tenets" of the Reformed faith. This means that we are not required to receive and adopt everything the confessions say. Remembering that they each reflect a particular time and a particular necessity, we acknowledge that they may at times vary from our current convictions. For example, the Scots Confession condemns the "error of the Anabaptists, who deny that children should be baptized before they have faith and understanding" (*Book of Confessions*, 3.23). And certain passages of the Westminster Confession of Faith (ch. X), felt to contain inferences that called for a more explicit statement of faith, were clarified by the church in 1903. Because the church is always being reformed by the Word of God, the confessions cannot be taken as a literal and complete statement of our present faith. These texts are not a straitjacket, binding our minds, but flags around which we may rally or anchors to steady the church against being "blown about with every wind of doctrine" (Eph. 4:14). When the church knows what it believes and can declare it clearly, it is in the strongest possible position to fulfill its Christian task.

A common theological thread runs through all the confessions despite differences in language, time of writing, and issues addressed. There are major themes in Reformed doctrine that are identified in the Foundations of Presbyterian Polity (F-2.05) and that may be considered "essential tenets." Central to the Reformed tradition is the "affirmation of the majesty, holiness, and providence of God." God is above all, through all, and in all. Nothing is beyond the concern and the love of God.

1. "The election of the people of God for service as well as for salvation." We are called as a people by God, and to respond in faith is to serve God and do God's will in the whole earth.

2. "Covenant life marked by a disciplined concern for order in the church according to the Word of God." We are a community of people bound together by God to keep the church faithful from age to age. This task informs the nature of our life together.

3. "A faithful stewardship that shuns ostentation and seeks proper use of the gifts of God's creation." The world is a part of God's good creation, and the faithful are stewards of this household (*oikumene*). As such we are responsible to God to live simply and in harmony with one another and the world.

4. "The recognition of the human tendency to idolatry and tyranny, which calls the people of God to work for the transformation of society by seeking justice and living in obedience to the Word of God." As obedient servants, we stand with God against all oppression and injustice. Our ordination sets us apart to serve with others as equals before the loving God who calls us to service.

The third ordination question is an important supplement to the first two. We fulfill our ordered ministry through obedience to Jesus Christ; this is first and central. We do so under the authority of the Scriptures, which bear witness to the lordship of Christ. We are guided by the confessions as reliable expositions of Scripture. Our confessions lead and instruct us as we seek to be faithful servants of God through Jesus Christ and under the power of the Holy Spirit.

Chapter 3

What Must a Ruling Elder Be?

*F*aith and character are intimately related. What we believe is reflected in our lives, and, conversely, what we do has determinative influence on our faith. Our lives speak far more convincingly than our words. The Form of Government states that all persons called to ordered ministries of the church—deacons, teaching elders, and ruling elders—should be "persons of strong faith, dedicated discipleship, and love of Jesus Christ as Savior and Lord. Their manner of life should be a demonstration of the Christian gospel in the church and in the world" (G-2.0104a). It is important that ruling elders be worthy people, but how do we gauge fitness of character?

If we look at those Jesus chose to be with him, we probably would not pick many of them as elders! There was Peter, emotionally volcanic, unpredictable, capable of great loyalty and courage, yet one who cringed before a servant and violently denied his discipleship; he was also slow to acknowledge the faith of Gentiles and vacillated in his convictions regarding the freedom and privileges of his new faith. There was Matthew, a tax gatherer, whose odious profession had dishonored him among his own people. Judas had a fatal flaw that was not apparent on the surface of his life. Neither these nor the other disciples were perfect persons, yet they were the ones Jesus chose, and what was accomplished through them is a marvel and a miracle.

Reflect for a moment on what Jesus accomplished through Peter. Matthew's Gospel records Jesus as saying to Peter, "You are Peter, and on this rock I will build my church" (Matt. 16:18). Can a more important role be imagined? The incidents that transpired in the Christian community immediately after the death and resurrection of Jesus, as related in the early chapters of Acts, show a strong and stable Peter as guide, counselor, and spokesperson for the whole group. Peter was the central figure in the church at Jerusalem, wisely guiding the infant church through times of crisis, internal friction, and external danger. He did, indeed, become a rock in a crucial time when a less courageous and committed disciple would have failed to meet the need of the hour.

This observation should serve to encourage a person who is asked to be a ruling elder to accept the invitation and not be too concerned about being "worthy." It is perhaps inevitable that anyone called by God to exercise leadership in the church should hesitate to respond at once to the summons. The spiritual demands of the task make anyone feel inadequate. This is characteristic even of persons in the Bible. When God summoned Moses from the burning bush to deliver the people from the hand of Pharaoh, his response was, "Who am I that I should go to Pharaoh, and bring the Israelites out of Egypt?" (Exod. 3:11). When Isaiah had a vision of God in the temple, he realized his unworthiness and at the same time exalted that he had been permitted to see the God who was calling him to service: "Woe is me!" he cried. "I am lost, for I am a man of unclean lips . . . yet my eyes have seen the King, the Lord of hosts!" (Isa. 6:5). Jeremiah lamented his youth and weakness when called by God to be a messenger. But in each case, God gave assurance that grace would be sufficient to make them useful servants of God—and all of them performed conspicuous service.

So if our immediate reaction to the invitation to be a ruling elder is, "I'm not the person for the job; there must be others better fitted for it," we are following a familiar pattern. But the matter should not end there, for that is where the conversation really begins! What personal qualifications fit one for the duties of this ordered ministry? "Am I 'spiritual' enough?" "I'm the trustee type; I feel at home in the business world and am confident in the sort of decision-making that requires. But I'm uncertain about being a ruling elder." "I believe in the church, but I'm not a person who prays a lot. Doesn't a ruling elder have to do that?"

Perhaps we can arrive at a clearer understanding of what a ruling elder must be if we approach the question under two heads: the ruling elder's qualifications as a Christian and a church member and the special qualifications for ordered ministry in the church.

Qualifications as a Christian and a Church Member

The sixth ordination question asks, "Will you in your own life seek to follow the Lord Jesus Christ, love your neighbors, and work for the reconciliation of the world?" (W-4.4003f). It is assumed that the ruling elder will be a Christian. It is difficult to define precisely what makes a person a Christian—we may be arbitrarily too sharp or too vague in drawing the picture—but let us make an attempt.

A Christian is a committed person. The life of the Christian belongs to Jesus Christ. The Christian has heard the message of God's love revealed in Jesus Christ and has realized that this love lays claim to his or her own life. The apostle Paul expressed it this way: "I appeal to you therefore, brothers and sisters, by the mercies of God, to present your bodies as a living sacrifice, holy and acceptable to God, which is your spiritual worship. Do not be conformed to this world but be transformed by the renewal of your minds, so that you may discern what is the will of God—what is good and acceptable and perfect" (Rom. 12:1–2). A twofold response is involved in this appeal, both a firm initial decision—"present your bodies as a living sacrifice"—and a consequent development of the spiritual life—"be transformed by the renewal of your minds." These two are joined to each other. We cannot present our bodies as a living sacrifice without going on to a daily surrender of our minds and hearts to the Spirit of God, by which we come to see and feel and act from a point of view very different from that which characterizes the world that is not under the rule of Christ. We need to remember here that Paul implied more than the physical body. He refers to one's personality at its fullest and most effective embodiment and expression; it is the whole person who is dedicated to Christ.

We may change the metaphor from sacrifice to citizenship. When we understand our status as Christians, we shall know that we have changed our citizenship; our subjection is no longer to the world of false ideals, wrong objectives, and unworthy motives by which we were once influenced. Our loyalty is now to Christ and Christ's rule in everything. It is this decision to let the will of God as revealed in Jesus Christ determine every aspect of life that makes a person a Christian. It calls for worship and obedience; it results in the transformation of character, whereby we are less and less imitators of the world and the "worldly" and more and more living expressions of God's Spirit.

As we reflect on all this, it becomes obvious that a ruling elder is more than a good person, a rigorously ethical or even a kind and generous person. A ruling elder is a Christian, and there is a difference. The difference is in one's faithfulness to God. There are many people who are model citizens, honest in business, cordial in relationships, community-minded, and advocates of right living. But essential to being a Christian is the awareness that a conversation is constantly taking place between the person and God, and that the person's part in the conversation leads to worship, repentance, commitment, and new life. A Christian may or may not be morally better than others, but whatever the Christian does will be done in the awareness that it is done in the sight of God. When the Christian does wrong, he or she recognizes that this is more than breaking a law. It is that, in the words of the psalmist, "Against you, you alone, have I sinned, and done what is evil in your sight" (Ps. 51:4). For the Christian, sin is a personal breach of loyalty.

By the same token, "righteousness" is not just correct character, but grateful trust in God, who loves us, and an acceptance of God's will for our lives. Character inevitably grows out of our faith, but it is not a substitute for faith. So ruling elders will wish to grow in their experience of God. Worship, both private and corporate, will be a valued practice. Reading and studying the Scripture will be a part of their discipline. Their lives will be constantly seeking to give the Spirit control over all their words and deeds.

There may be moments when ruling elders, like all persons, feel despair in their attempts to achieve praiseworthy spiritual lives, even as Paul confessed that he had not attained (Phil. 3:12). But elders will be useful to God nevertheless if they persist as did the apostle when he wrote, "Forgetting what lies behind and straining forward to what lies ahead, I press toward the goal for the prize of the heavenly call of God in Christ Jesus" (Phil. 3:13–14).

Qualifications for Ordered Ministry

One would hope that what has just been said would constitute sufficient qualifications for election to ruling elder. Those who were chosen as leaders of the early church were described as persons "of good standing, full of the Spirit and of wisdom" (Acts 6:3), which implies that they were esteemed by the community, deeply and sincerely religious in spirit, and practical in judgment. Yet there is something more required of a ruling elder. This quality is hard to define and may be said to be included in what we refer to as "leadership."

A ruling elder is a member of a team. Ordination question eight asks, "Will you pray for and seek to serve the people with energy, intelligence, imagination, and love?" (W-4.4003h). The ruling elder must be cooperative and flexible. Firm convictions and strong initiative are desirable qualities if they do not lead to self-assertion or unbending insistence on one's own opinions. The Holy Spirit exercises leadership for the fullest advantage to the church when working through committed individuals as members of a group. Our church government is based on a Spirit-filled community that chooses competent persons to represent them in the spiritual ordering of the life of the church. "Ruling elders, together with teaching elders, exercise leadership, government, spiritual discernment, and discipline and have responsibilities for the life of a congregation as well as the whole church, including ecumenical relationships" (G-2.0301). When the elders meet as a session, they meet as Spirit-filled persons where private judgments will be either confirmed by the consent of the rest or corrected in the light that falls from other minds. This does not mean that the group is always right and the individual always wrong; but the government and discipline of the Presbyterian Church are firmly based on the conviction that the Spirit of God speaks to and through the whole church, and not to special persons ecclesiastically qualified. This principle also pervades a session meeting, and however right an elder may think he or she is, if his or her individuality disrupts the group spirit, the ordered ministry of elders is not helpfully fulfilled. To be able to think with others, pray with others, and work with others is one of the qualifications of the elder.

In this relation, the seventh ordination question needs careful consideration: "Do you promise to further the peace, unity, and purity of the Church?" (W-4.4003g). The ruling elder is pledged to "further the peace . . . of the church." Peace is more than the absence of conflict. It is not a static condition in which affairs simply go on without change or variation. World peace is more than nations living quietly within set boundaries and disturbing each other as little as possible. It is never possible that this be true in a world of relentless change. Rather, peace is dynamic; it is purposeful and creative change. When we see leaders in politics, in business, and in related groups retooling economic policies and revamping national and international agreements and laws in the light of changing conditions and for the good of all the earth's people, that is a picture of world peace. The "peace of the church" is the church in creative action as it earnestly seeks to understand its mission and to fulfill it.

Thus the session is a body of believers open to change. Peace in the church is an alert congregation joyously and energetically fulfilling its mission as Christ's agent in the world. To study how this may happen is a concern of the ruling elder.

Obviously there can be no peace where there is not unity. Paul pleads with the Christians at Philippi to complete his joy in Christ by being "of the same mind, having the same love, being in full accord and of one mind" (Phil. 2:2). He cites the example of Jesus as one who sought unity of spirit. As Jesus "emptied himself" of heavenly status and glory to take the form of a servant and even to die a shameful death on a cross, so the Christian must do nothing from conceit or selfishness, but be humble and look for the best interests of others (Phil. 2:3–7). No influence toward unity is more powerful in a church than this spirit demonstrated by the session. On the other hand, jealousy, hurt feelings, personal ambition, or party loyalties serve to mar the unity that the Holy Spirit would engender among ruling elders and in the congregation. It is equally sad when division occurs between pastor and session. No quarrels are quite as damaging as religious quarrels because so much seems at stake. Yet this need not be true. Elders need not all hold the same opinion on matters of concern to the church, but they must pray earnestly for forgiveness and reconciliation that the Holy Spirit may be sent into their hearts to bring peace and love. To "maintain the unity of the Spirit in the bonds of peace" (Eph. 4:3) is incumbent upon every elder.

Lastly, the ruling elder promises to study the "purity of the church." This implies that the church may be corrupted, and history bears out this sad truth. The ruling elder will stand guard to see that the church is not corrupted in either its doctrine or its spirit, for from these come corruption in action.

The Presbyterian Church is a creedal church and regards right doctrine as being of great importance. For the believer, the creeds and confessions are road maps; they help us find our way. They are not the way itself, any more than a road map is the road. But travelers need maps, and a faulty map is an unhappy deception. We are zealous for right teaching because we believe that the way of salvation through Jesus Christ can be described plainly enough that the seeker can find adequate help. But a caution must be inserted here: just as a road map must from time to time be revised to bring it into line with the real and changing roads (we will not press the analogy any farther, as that would imply that the "way of salvation" changes), so theologies must be studied and restated to bring them into conformity with the contemporary understanding of God's dealing with us for our well-being. Theologies are important, as are road maps, but they are the products of human thought about God's continuing self-revelation. So our attitude in defense of pure doctrine will be a reverent and humble teachableness in the revelation of God's will with a firm purpose to understand and define it as clearly as possible in light of what has gone before and what is taking place at the present time. The word of God, speaking by the Spirit through the Scriptures, is the standard for purity of doctrine. This message, as found in the creeds and confessions of the *Book of Confessions*, unites Presbyterians in their search for purity of doctrine.

The purity of the church must be defended in its life as in its doctrine. The church exists in and for God's world, a world that the Scriptures warn is both deceived and deceiver. Jesus refused to be enticed by the blandishments of the world and challenged his disciples to do likewise. That the church is "in but not of" the world is an important distinction. We are called to be holy as the Lord is holy.

This is not the place to discuss worldliness at length. The views of church people through the centuries have changed remarkably from generation to generation about what constitutes worldliness. Differing views will be held by the members of any session. Worldliness is far more subtle than the recognition that there are practices with which we disagree. We are able to distinguish overt "sins" and to combat them more or less effectively. The fact that many in the church, and outside it, live unimpeachable lives blinds us to the real presence of the spirit of evil in the world that we are called by the pure spirit of Christ to combat. "The kingdom of evil," writes John Oman,

is idolatry, so organized by hypocrisy that it is able to set itself up as the true order of the world. Valuing its neighbor only for itself, it makes possession the end and humankind the means, and turns the whole world into a temple for its idol, where it worships with all its mind and with all its heart and with all its strength. By the dazzling liturgy of all the worldly interests that appeal to selfish desire, it blinds its own eyes as well as the eyes of others, till its idol is accepted as the only true might in the world, over against which a rule of love seems mere fantasy and cloud-land. Nor did this idolatry ever erect a ritual so imposing as the material conquests of the present order of competition with its vast material equipment; nor was it ever so much taken at its face value as when thus enormously staged; nor has society ever been set by it on a more selfish foundation or been so robbed of the true uses of the world; nor has it ever issued in vaster destruction. (John Oman, *Grace and Reality*, 4th ed. [Cambridge, MA: Cambridge University Press, 1931], 34)

Professor Oman's characterization of the reign of evil bears pondering by ruling elders. What are truly our concerns for the purity of the church? How much time and energy do we spend arguing about what constitutes evil practices to the exclusion of the deeper concerns of greed, oppression, injustice, and warfare that are currently tearing apart the fabric of peace, both in the church and in the world? How willing are we to "bear the cross" of being misunderstood, opposed, or even vilified when we insist on probing deep enough to begin to root out the underlying causes of the world's unrest and injustices that have their foundation in alienation from God's will for peace and shalom?

Those who call themselves disciples must dare to drink of the cup from which Christ drank and receive the baptism with which he was baptized. We must face boldly the challenges of worldliness and not let ourselves live a worldly life of comfort under the illusion that we are still Christian. May God spare us the easy pleasure of having escaped the shattering judgment of Christ's cross by which alone the sham of this world's pretension is exposed. A book by the great Danish philosopher Soren Kierkegaard is titled *Purity of Heart Is to Will One Thing*. The psalmist cried, "one thing I asked of the Lord, that will I seek after" (Ps. 27:4). Purity in the church comes through single-minded dedication to its Lord.

Chapter 4

The Session

"*T*he session is the council for the congregation. It shall be composed of those persons elected by the congregation to active service as ruling elders, together with all installed pastors and associate pastors. . . . The session shall have responsibility for governing the congregation . . ." (G-3.0201). The Form of Government then lists eighteen specific duties and responsibilities of the session, ranging from receiving and dismissing members to providing for their worship and nurture, including the nurture and spiritual growth of members of the session itself, to the continuing relationship with other councils in the denomination and, beyond, to global and ecumenical relationships. Thus the duties of the session are many and varied. Responsibilities sometimes called administrative, in order to distinguish them from those thought of as spiritual, are linked by the constitution in such a way as to enhance the spiritual dimension of all that the session does. Responsibility for budgets, property, maintenance, salaries, and program supervision are recognized as requiring gifts of the Holy Spirit, just as the ministry of the ruling elder is understood to be a part of the whole ministry of the people of God.

One of the great satisfactions of serving on the session is the opportunity to establish lasting friendships with others of like dedication and purpose. Women and men who serve as ruling elders find that this service affords them the chance to share in deep and significant ways with their peers on the session and to grow in the knowledge and love of God and their associates in ministry.

The size of the session will differ with each congregation and is usually determined by the manner in which the congregation does its work and by the numerical strength of the membership. While the Form of Government is the same for all Presbyterian churches, the constitution does not specify either the size of the session or how it is to be organized. These details are left to the discretion of each congregation and to the ruling elders who have been chosen by it. The Form of Government does specify that a quorum "shall include the moderator and either a specific number of ruling elders or a specific percentage of those ruling elders in current service on the session" (G-3.0203). To ensure that membership on the session is truly representative, the Form of Government provides two safeguards. One safeguard is the requirement that the session "give full expression to the rich diversity of the church's membership and shall provide for full participation and access to representation in decision-making and employment practices" and that the session "shall develop procedures and mechanisms for promoting and reviewing that body's implementation of the church's commitment to inclusiveness and representation" (G-3.0103). The other safeguard is a rotating system of active service for ruling elders and deacons. If a church finds it difficult to provide a rotation of terms (due, for example, to limited membership), it may make a written request that the presbytery, by majority vote, grant a waiver of this limitation on terms (G-2.0404).

The Form of Government requires that there always be three classes of ruling elders on the session and three classes of deacons on the board of deacons. "However, no ruling elder or deacon shall be eligible to serve more than six consecutive years, and a ruling elder or deacon who has served six consecutive years shall be ineligible for election to the same board for at least one year" (G-2.0404). Terms shall ordinarily be for three years, and eligibility for reelection is determined by congregational rule. The pastor of the church is the moderator of the session. In churches where there are copastors, they shall both be considered moderators and make provisions for who presides at a particular meeting. However, there may be occasions when it is prudent for the pastor not to moderate the session. In such cases the pastor "shall invite another teaching elder who is a member of the presbytery or a person authorized by the presbytery to serve as moderator" (G-3.0104). If the pastor is ill or absent, the same expedient may be adopted. The sessions of churches without an installed pastor are moderated by a teaching elder appointed by the presbytery. One of the compelling reasons for these regulations is that they preserve the unity and interconnected nature of the councils of the Presbyterian Church. The teaching elder is a member of presbytery and, as such, serves to facilitate the relationship of the congregation with the larger church. At the same time, neither pastor nor session can exercise authority without the other. Together they form, under Christ, the authority necessary to discharge their responsibility for the spiritual government of the congregation.

The pastor may call a meeting of the session whenever he or she deems it necessary and must do so when requested in writing by any two members of the session. The session also meets when directed to do so by the presbytery. In any event, the session is required by the constitution to hold stated meetings at least quarterly. (G-3.0203)

In order that the business of the session shall proceed in an orderly fashion, a docket is usually prepared. This is often done by the clerk, in consultation with the pastor, and should anticipate all matters that need to come before the session. Since the session is charged with maintaining the mission and government of the congregation, various areas of responsibility ought to come regularly before it for prayerful consideration. Proper planning and procedure are necessary if the whole life of the church is to produce a body of Christians "mature in Christ." And since the congregation is an inseparable part of the denomination, the concerns of both local and worldwide mission need due consideration.

A docket for a meeting of the session might contain the following items:

1. Opening prayer
2. Taking the roll
3. Reading and approval of the minutes
4. Communications from presbytery, synod, and General Assembly
5. Reports of permanent and special committees
6. Report of the pastor(s)
7. Report of the clerk
8. Report of the treasurer
9. Examination and reception of new members and/or dismissal of members
10. Arrangements for the Lord's Supper and baptism when necessary
11. Report to presbytery (when in order)
12. Reports of commissioners to other councils
13. Unfinished business
14. Other new or miscellaneous business
15. Adjournment with prayer and benediction

Following the opening prayer, the first items of business fall to the clerk. The clerk is a ruling elder, elected to the office by the session. The responsibilities of the clerk include keeping an accurate record of attendance, recording the minutes of session meetings and meetings of the congregation, issuing letters of transfer, reporting to other councils as required, transmitting to the session communications from other councils and ecumenical agencies, and supervising and maintaining the required registers of church membership. Keeping the roll of the session means recording both those present and those absent at each meeting. Minutes are read to ensure accuracy before they are permanently entered into the minute book and are examined each year by the presbytery.

The docket also indicates reports of permanent and special committees. In a smaller church, the session often acts as a committee of the whole to transact its business, but in most cases there will be work that has been assigned to committees, some of which will have members from the congregation at large as well as from the session. The session cannot do all the work of the church. It should divide, assign, and oversee the total program, in which everyone carries part of the load. But policy and direction are the prerogatives of the session, and committee reports often make up a large part of the agenda of a session meeting.

Permanent committees carry responsibility for various phases of the continuing program of the church, while special committees are constituted for a particular task and dissolved when the task is completed. Since no two churches or communities are alike, no single committee structure will work equally well everywhere. The mission of the church is one, but the way in which it is done will vary from place to place and from time to time. Yet every session bears similar responsibilities, and some suggestions may be made about organization that can be adapted by almost any session.

1. The prime responsibility of the session is to assist the pastor in the oversight of the spiritual welfare of the congregation. This shepherding role may well be carried out by the session as a whole. One of the session's responsibilities is "reviewing the roll of active members at least annually and counseling with those who have neglected the responsibilities of membership" (G-3.0201c). The church is more than a congregation of individuals. By precept and example the session must seek to achieve an organism in which every member finds meaning and usefulness in relation to the whole and matures in a life of prayer and the spirit.

In a smaller congregation where "everybody knows everybody," the care of the congregation may be relatively simple: new members will be made welcome, the sick will be visited, friendship will be encouraged among the people, and family and personal crises will be met with loving support. In an urban church or a large congregation, care of the members will be a heavier responsibility and will require intentional organization to achieve. The parish may be divided into geographical sections, with ruling elders and deacons assigned the responsibility to encourage and develop teams of members who will report when people leave the community, visit in cases of illness or need, help assimilate new members, arrange for home meetings for prayer and study, and otherwise provide for Christian fellowship among members. This is an invaluable service to pastors who cannot maintain this sort of relationship with a large membership. The pastors can be informed by ruling elders of those needing pastoral care.

2. The session has the responsibility and power to "provide that the Word of God may be truly preached and heard" and to "provide that the Sacraments may be rightly administered and received" (G-3.0201a, b). Worship is the very heart of the Christian community, the one indispensable function of the people of God. It is therefore a primary duty of the session not only to provide occasions for worship but also to persuade the people of its importance and encourage them in regular attendance. While the ruling elders may properly expect that the teaching elder is best qualified to lead congregational worship, it is by no means the pastor's responsibility alone. Pastors will seek the counsel and support of the session in planning to carry out this aspect of the church's ministry. There should be a committee on worship to which other members of the congregation may be coopted. This committee will work with the pastor(s) and the professional musicians, if any, in all aspects of the church's worship: the music program, choosing and training ushers, the schedule and preparation for the sacraments, the order and times of worship, and provision for filling the pulpit in the absence of the pastor. Training in the art of worship, in order that persons of all ages may participate meaningfully, is also a concern of the session.

3. The Christian education program of the church is also under the supervision of the session. The Form of Government refers to the session's duty to provide "programs of nurture, education, and fellowship" and to lead the congregation "in participating in the mission of the whole church" (G-3.0201c). The church is a community of learners seeking to discern the movement of faith and the meaning of ministry. Membership is composed of persons of all ages and may include persons with various mental and physical abilities and persons of various ethnic and cultural backgrounds. Christian nurture must encompass spiritual growth and knowledge of Christian history and heritage, the content and teaching of the Bible, and the development of the ability to make ethical decisions and to work for the kingdom's goals of justice and peace for all humankind.

A Christian education committee will help the session to plan and carry out the responsibility for the varied aspects of the church's educational ministry. Among the duties of the committee will be leadership recruitment and training; recommending and planning educational programs for all ages, including youth and young adult programs; concerns for the aging and those with special needs; family life emphases; stewardship education; an understanding of and commitment to the global mission of the church; preparation for study, reflection, and action in the community and beyond on issues facing the Christian in the world; recommendations for educational materials; and the coordination of the educational program of the congregation with its worship and service. An enthusiastic and well-informed committee can transform the character of the church and its ministry.

4. The session will also be concerned with the finances of the church. It has the responsibility of "encouraging the graces of generosity and faithful stewardship of personal and financial resources" (G-3.0201c). The session is also charged with adopting a budget, determining the distribution of the congregation's benevolences, and accounting for all offerings and disbursements: "It shall provide full information to the congregation concerning its decisions in such matters" (G-3.0205). This responsibility may be handled in a variety of ways. A finance committee of the session may be formed, especially in those churches that do not have trustees. In those instances where a board of trustees exists, the session must nevertheless supervise their work. A joint committee may facilitate this task. In any case, the session cannot delegate its responsibility for the benevolences of the congregation. A committee on benevolence may perform several duties: studying and informing the congregation of the benevolence needs of the General Assembly and other councils, proposing the share of financial support that the congregation will contribute, and providing programs of education and information in order that the congregation may respond intelligently and generously. The distinction sometimes made about the budget of the church where some portions are designated as "for ourselves" and other portions as "for others" is a doubtful one. We are a world church and our mission is one mission, whether carried out locally, nationally, or worldwide. The committee may seek the help of presbytery and ecumenical agencies as it seeks to enable the congregation to be faithful to the unity of the church and to its obligation to the larger fellowship of which it is a part.

The committees just mentioned are merely suggestions. Sessions may function effectively with more or fewer or different ones. In some churches the evangelistic effort is assigned to a committee; in others stewardship is made a special assignment, as is care of the property. Flexibility of organization is necessary if all situations are to be met and the needs of the congregation and the church at large are to be properly considered. What we have suggested here gives an indication of how a ruling elder may serve as a member of the session. Ruling elders will have responsibilities beyond serving on a committee or committees. These are described in the Form of Government (G-2.0301). An understanding of the nature and mission of the church is necessary, and learning about these will be a part of the continuing education of the ruling elders. Regular occasions for study and discussion of a wide range of topics related to the responsibilities of the ruling elder should be part of the ongoing work of the session.

The church believes that the will of God is revealed through the Holy Spirit in groups of Christians who thoughtfully and prayerfully wait on God for guidance. The session meeting should, therefore, provide for more than the business of the church; it should provide opportunity for spiritual growth of its members through worship and study. Ruling elders should be growing into the maturity that is in Christ. The church can go no faster and no further than the vision and knowledge of its leaders will permit. Sessions should engage in a process for education and mutual growth for their members. The educational agencies of the General Assembly have provided materials for preparing ruling elders for their responsibilities and personal growth, both before their ordination and on a continuing basis. Thus ruling elders may enlarge their insights into the nature of the church, deepen their loyalty to Christ by a clearer discernment of what Jesus means for personal faith and the world's salvation, and become more effective and enthusiastic workers as they see the part they play in the whole structure and program of the church.

Chapter 5

The Churches and the Church

*W*hen we think about organized Christianity (and has there ever been any other kind?), many of us will at once picture the particular church with which we are most familiar, probably the one to which we belong. We know it as a relatively small religious community carrying on its varied activities and often seeming to be complete in and of itself. It is busy in a full life of worship, fellowship, teaching, and service that have come to have value and meaning to members through their participation. To all intents and purposes it may appear autonomous in regulating its own affairs and in owning and maintaining its property. Some denominations, which are "congregational" in form of government, define the overall church as precisely all these individual churches entering voluntarily into cooperation with one another, without, however, involving any curtailment of the sovereignty that adheres by right in each congregation.

The Presbyterian idea is quite different. The local congregation is understood as a member within the organism that is the total church. Presbyterian churches are not independent and autonomous; each is related essentially and structurally to the larger body of which it is indissolubly a part. The Presbyterian Church and the churches are mutually involved in such a way that neither can exist without the other: one church, indivisible and universal, must exist in the churches; but it is the faith vitally experienced in the churches that gives reality and power to the church. Foundations of Presbyterian Polity states that "the particular congregations of the Presbyterian Church (U.S.A.) wherever they are, taken collectively, constitute one church, called the church" (F-3.0201). This may seem confusing at first, but it is the basic principle of Presbyterian government and discipline. The local congregation, although given a great deal of freedom in the determination of its affairs, is not autonomous. The constitution provides that this freedom is exercised within well-defined limits. A congregation cannot by itself call and install its choice of a pastor; it is the prerogative of the presbytery to participate in the search and to approve the call and install the pastor. Teaching elders hold membership in presbytery and not in the local church. The minutes of the session must be presented for examination to the presbytery, and all decisions and actions of the session and congregation may be reviewed by the presbytery. Presbytery has the ecclesiastical power to discipline a church, its session, or its pastor.

The Presbyterian Church is essentially one body, for we have one constitution, with a *Book of Order* and a *Book of*

Confessions, and one common program as defined by the whole church through its General Assembly. In reality, ours is a close-knit unity.

This unity is expressed through a representative form of government. Each congregation, through its session, is represented in the presbytery by a commissioner or commissioners. In turn, on a ratio basis and by a balanced number of ruling and teaching elders, each presbytery elects representatives to attend synod and the General Assembly. This is the most inclusive council of our denomination, with jurisdiction extending over the entire church. This system of government should not seem strange to us in the United States, for in many respects there is a remarkable parallel between our civil government and that of our church. Local units of government—towns, counties, and states—approximate congregations, presbyteries, and synods; and the federal government, functioning through legislative, administrative, and judicial branches, approximates the General Assembly with its various agencies and units. This form of government expresses the unity and solidarity of the whole yet makes ample room for local independence and initiative. How does this affect the ruling elder who serves in the session of a local church?

We have seen that the session is responsible for the benevolence program of the congregation. Every congregation that is worthy of the name of a Christian church should be doing something for others. It is a service agency carrying out the will of Christ. Its areas of concern are not limited to its own life but extend to the surrounding community and to the wider needs of the nation and the world. No church that is not growing in the range of its vision and outreach will increase spiritual vitality within itself. Encouraging the church in obedience to its Lord to undertake tasks beyond its own walls and to propose ways and means by which this may be accomplished can be the most exciting and stimulating aspect of the work of an elder.

A notable New Testament scholar, speaking of the mission of the church, has said that its life and work should be a continuation of that which Jesus began to do in his short ministry on earth. In fact, when we understand the church truly, it is itself a manifestation in the world of the present activity of the living Christ working through the Holy Spirit. The Gospels make it clear that Jesus conceived his work to be to preach the gospel of God, to teach the meaning of that gospel in relation to life, and to use his Spirit-given power to heal and help the needy. The church has always understood its mission in terms that it believed Christ had commissioned: "Go therefore and make disciples of all nations . . . teaching them to obey everything that I have commanded you. And remember, I am with you always, to the end of the age" (Matt. 28:19–20). The God-given tasks of the church are thus to include evangelism, teaching, and service in the name of Christ.

To this end the General Assembly has created various agencies, responsible to it, which plan and administer programs for the whole church and which aid the congregations and councils together to carry out the one mission of the church. Among these agencies are those whose major responsibility is for programs and ministries of education and nurture. Study courses for children, youth, and adults are prepared for the church. The development of leaders, including teachers, pastors, educators, ruling elders, and deacons, is assisted through strategies, programs, support, and materials fashioned in cooperation with councils. Conferences are supported for various groups in the church. Cooperation with colleges, universities, and seminaries helps to ensure their support and the continuation of high standards of academic and religious achievement. In short, wherever there is an evident need for teaching in any part of the church, the services of its agencies of education are called on.

To meet the challenge of making disciples, both at home and around the globe, the General Assembly, in cooperation with other councils and ecumenical institutions, supports and encourages programs of evangelism. To make Jesus Christ known to the world's people is a constant concern. Where there exist cooperative bodies such as councils of churches, cooperation makes possible a united approach to common problems. The unity of the church of Jesus Christ compels Presbyterians to work with others of like mind and concern in efforts to witness to the gospel through word and deed.

Other ministries related to the General Assembly assist the church in its outreach to those in need at home and abroad. Schools, hospitals, agriculture programs, health, justice, and education are concerns that, along with telling the good news, accompany our mission efforts. Starting new churches as well as redeveloping those that have fallen on hard times is a part of the outreach of the church through General Assembly action. Because of our deep commitment to the diversity of the church in its unity, the Assembly provides leadership, funding, programs, and resources that make the enrichment of the total church possible through the contributions of those of differing racial and ethnic origins. The church speaks in a variety of tongues, and the mosaic of its life is full of the colors of all of God's races.

The work of the church is one work. The U.S. church receives mission endeavors from other countries and seeks to learn more about its life and work from those sent to us by other churches. Mission workers from the worldwide church bring new opportunities for ministry and mission to churches in every part of the world. Further, the Presbyterian Church contributes to world Christianity through active participation in such alliances as the World Council of Churches and the World Communion of Reformed Churches. Well-developed programs of global and ecumenical education are needed in each local church. The General Assembly agencies provide information and often make available the services of missionary personnel.

Nor does the church forget its servants who have labored long and faithfully in its service. Pension systems have been devised to provide retirement income for church workers and to offer emergency assistance in many areas such as health and education. Homes for the aged and relief for the widowed are also part of the church's pension system.

Other areas of concern addressed at the General Assembly level include theological education and relationships with the seminaries of the denomination; the development of worship and liturgical aids and education; keeping the church informed about social issues and recommending action to ease social, economic, and justice ills; racial and ethnic concerns; and programs for women and men in the church.

The persons who make up these agencies are elected by the General Assembly from congregations and councils across the church. They are created by the General Assembly—that is, by women and men from local congregations who gather as the Assembly—and through prayerful consideration of the life of the church and the issues facing it, and led by the Holy Spirit, they make decisions about programs, budgets, priorities, and directions. The agencies are not autonomous; they report to the General Assembly and their policies are determined by Assembly-elected boards. They are staffed by dedicated women and men who consider their work a ministry to which God has called them and in which they serve, as do all servants of Jesus Christ.

This has been a very rapid review of the Presbyterian way of responding to the commission of Christ. At every level, ruling elders may be called on to render service. Ruling elders should consider service rendered to councils beyond the session as a joyous opportunity to serve the church of Christ. Meetings of presbytery and other councils are places where the ministry of the church is debated and implemented. Presbyters (ruling elders and teaching elders) are part of the governance of a denomination that is not sectarian in its point of view—that is, it does not hold a narrow or exclusivist concept of the Christian faith but is true to the broad spirit and to the ancient and modern creeds of the world church. Presbyterians are eager to work with other Christians in promoting the essential unity of the church of Christ. It is our prayer that all may be one, in spirit and witness if not in name, even as Christ desired, together bringing healing, peace, and unity to a broken world. Ruling elders are privileged to witness and serve in such a church.

Chapter 6

The Session and the Pastor

"*F*rom Miletus he sent a message to Ephesus, asking the elders of the church to meet him" (Acts 20:17). The strong bond of fellowship between the elders in the church at Ephesus and the apostle Paul reminds us of the unique relation between the session and the pastor. The parallel is not exact, for the apostle was not a settled minister in a parish. Yet on the occasion of a prolonged visit to the city during the course of a missionary journey, he doubtless had opportunity for extended collaboration, from which grew the mutual esteem and love so movingly depicted in the incident described by Luke. There is no other enterprise in the world in which persons are so drawn to one another and to the leader as in the labor that ruling elders and pastors undertake for their Lord and Savior. Friendship naturally develops where persons are thrown together in common endeavors, and it may be unusually firm under special circumstances. But the bond of pastor and ruling elders is based on the communion that Christ creates by his Spirit. It was described by Jesus when he said to his disciples:

> You are my friends if you do what I command you. I do
> not call you servants any longer, because the servant does
> not know what the master is doing; but I have called you
> friends, because I have made known to you everything
> that I have heard from my Father. You did not choose me
> but I chose you. And I appointed you to go and bear fruit,
> fruit that will last, so that the Father will give you what-
> ever you ask him in my name. I am giving you these com-
> mands so that you may love one another. (John 15:14–17)

There are unhappy exceptions to the rule, as might be
expected among persons who are far from perfect. But
rare is the situation in which a pastor does not refer to the
ruling elders with pride and affection; conversely, ruling
elders speak of their pastor in equally warm terms.

The spirit of mutual regard and unity is not something
that just happens. It must be cultivated. A few suggestions
may be helpful in achieving this end.

1. As an expression of Christian principle, the adage
"good fences make good neighbors" leaves much to be
desired. Yet it does point to the truth that each of two par-
ties must know and honor mutual rights and privileges if
good relations are to be maintained. While it is a techni-
cal point, both pastors and ruling elders should know the
limits of their respective authority and should not intrude
on spheres assigned to others. For example, some tasks
a pastor shares equally with ruling elders. Indeed, in the
exercise of spiritual rule in the church, teaching elders

and ruling elders are both called presbyters. As presbyters, the teaching elder and the ruling elder share equal authority; their votes count the same in presbytery and other councils. This parity is further emphasized by the fact that teaching elders and ruling elders together comprise the session, and no action taken by either unilaterally is officially valid. But in other ways a teaching elder stands in a unique relationship, both to the session and to the congregation. The pastor is a member of the presbytery and not the congregation in which he or she serves. Further, the pastor is installed in the church by the presbytery, to which is reserved the power to remove him or her from it. Changes in the salary of the pastor must be approved by presbytery. Thus it is evident that neither the session nor the congregation exercises authority over the pastor. It ought also to be understood that the authority of the pastor in the church does not rest in the person. In the Presbyterian order of church government, the presbytery exercises the office of bishop, with oversight of each congregation, and the pastor is really the representative of presbytery, commissioned to serve a particular congregation. This status gives the pastor considerable freedom, which under the authority of presbytery is used to preach the gospel in its purity and fullness and in love. A mutual respect for those provisions of the Form of Government will make for the "good neighborliness" which is so great a blessing.

2. The observations that have just been made are not intended to imply that the session, or an individual ruling elder, should not consult with the pastor about any matter concerning the church. Indeed, if the pastor is wise, the wisdom and guidance of the ruling elders and deacons will be welcome and sought. Every pastor can recall with gratitude instances where the sage counsel of an experienced Christian colleague has prevented a rash act, secured balance in judgment, or brought perspective in a confused situation. In helpful ways the session can be the line of communication between pastor and people. Who knows the congregation better than those elected by it? The session should have the concern and the courage to interpret the needs of the people to the pastor as it sees them, and the attitude of the pastor should be so receptive that such observations will never be construed as reproaches. On the other hand, who has better opportunity to know the pastor than those with whom the ordered ministry of ruling elder is shared? There will often be times when ruling elders may interpret to the people the hopes, dreams, anxieties, and points of view of the pastor. When it may be impossible or unseemly for the pastor to speak for herself or himself, members of the session who love and trust their pastor can effectively speak out. This mutual confidence and reciprocity is both the fruit of the Spirit's work and the condition of the Spirit's further operation. This is in large measure the secret of the fellowship of kindred minds.

3. No pastor who is sensitive to the proprieties of the call and who is unselfish in motive will divulge to the session or the congregation the happiness that a little thoughtfulness on their part would bring to the pastor and the pastor's family. While the pastor and members of his or her family are constantly with people, theirs is often a lonely task. The pastor bears the burdens of the flock, and the people may never know their weight. The pastor and the pastor's family have needs and emergencies, and ruling elders are in a better position than anyone else to know what these needs and burdens are. It is their privilege to help, individually as friends and collectively as the session. No pastor deliberately and openly seeks tokens of the people's appreciation and affection, yet pastors are human and need the warmth of personal friendships, which professional relationships cannot bring.

4. At each celebration of the Lord's Supper our memory is stirred by reflection on the presence of the Lord and the disciples at the Last Supper. This reflection is especially meaningful to teaching elders and ruling elders who unite in the performance of this sacrament. Even as the disciples in the upper room enjoyed a profound comradeship, so it is no presumption for teaching elders and ruling elders to seek the same at the Table. The Communion table is placed so that the family of faith may gather about it. The teaching elder officiates in the name of the unseen Lord, whose presence is no less real because it is "in the spirit." The teaching elder gives the elements to those who serve with him or her in the care of the people of God, who then distribute them to the gathered worshipers, as Jesus blessed, broke, and gave the bread through his disciples to the multitude. The unity in Christ between teaching elder and ruling elders is typified by their service at the Table. It is here that teaching elders and ruling elders dedicate themselves to serving the congregation. There is order, division of responsibility, and recognition of the value of the labors of each.

All that has been written in this book is based on the premise that to serve as ruling elder in the Presbyterian Church is an honor and a rewarding service. It is not the sort of honor desired by the world, where one receives praise and plaudits; rather, it is the satisfaction that comes when one is called by the Spirit through the voice of the church to serve Jesus Christ. The secret of effectiveness as a ruling elder will be dependence on God, a wholehearted commitment to one's responsibilities, and continuing growth. As ruling elders join in conferences and training experiences intended to promote the development of their gifts, as they sincerely study the will of God for their own lives and usefulness, as they faithfully carry out their duties to the people whose spiritual welfare is their concern, they will gain a sense of worth and enduring satisfaction. This is service that requires much and pays large dividends. May God bless all who are called to it.

CPSIA information can be obtained at www.ICGtesting.com
Printed in the USA
LVOW05s1427020714

392574LV00009B/182/P